Dear Future Husband

31 Days of Praying God's Blessing for the Spouse God has for you!

Cheryl L. Thomas

Copyright © 2017 Cheryl L. Thomas

All Rights Reserved. No part of this book may be reproduced in any form or by any electronic or mechanical means, including information storage and retrieval systems, without permission in writing from the publisher, except by a reviewer, who may quote brief passages in a review.

Scripture quotations are taken from the King James Version (KJV) of the Bible except where noted. Public Domain.

Scripture quotations marked (NIV) are taken from the Holy Bible, New International Version®, NIV®. Copyright © 1973, 1978, 1984, 2011 by Biblica, Inc.™ Used by permission of Zondervan. All rights reserved worldwide. www.zondervan.com The "NIV" and "New International Version" are trademarks registered in the United States Patent and Trademark Office by Biblica, Inc.™

Published by:

Be Books

P.O. Box 6103
Gainesville, Florida 32627

◼ Dedication

I'd like to dedicate this book to every single Christian woman patiently waiting for her future husband to make his entrance into her life.

I know the waiting has been long. I know at times frustration levels get high. But through experiencing the prayers in this short devotional, I pray that you'll turn your heart, attention and prayers to the one who needs them most – your future husband.

Don't fret. He's coming!

Introduction:

A year from now, I'll be 50 years old. That's right – half a century. Never in my wildest imagination could anyone have ever convinced me that I wouldn't be married with a gaggle of children by now.

Throughout all these years, I've spent countless hours daydreaming about my future husband. I've laughed and cried with friends about the characteristics I wanted my future husband to have. I've argued with family members about my lengthy must-have list for my future husband. And, I've talked with men I've dated about the qualities they needed to exhibit to be my future husband.

But through all of that daydreaming, discussion, laughter, arguments and pointless talks, I found that I missed a truly important element. I'd never really ***prayed*** for my future husband.

Oh, don't get me wrong. I certainly complained to God about why He was taking so long in sending my future husband. I'd begged God to speed up the husband-making process and I'd whined to Him about my perception of the men I'd been dating, but I can't say that I had ever sincerely prayed *for* him. Ever.

Now, I'm not talking about praying that he would come soon. I did that. I'm not talking about praying what he would look like. I did that. I'm not talking about praying for things that don't matter. I did that, too.

But praying **_for_** HIM? Never. I'd NEVER prayed for his soul, prayed for his vision, prayed for his purpose. Never had I prayed for his health, his wealth, his joy, his relationship with God and others.

So God led me to pray **_for_** him. And I did. Enclosed in these pages you'll find 31 simple but powerful prayers of a woman praying for the man God is preparing for her as that same God is preparing her for him.

Some of the prayers are short and impactful, some longer; some of them are slightly humorous, some sober and sincere. But they are all heartfelt prayers coming from the soul of a woman preparing not to just spend moments praying for her future husband, but preparing her heart to spend a lifetime lifting up his concerns to their God.

I pray that as you read and meditate on my simple prayers to God for my future husband, that God begins to whisper prayers in your heart for YOUR future husband. I hope you are inspired to pray for his future, pray for his destiny, pray for his heart, pray for his soul, pray for his spiritual wellbeing, pray for his emotional wellbeing, his social wellbeing, and his financial wellbeing. I hope your prayers *about* him, as mine once were, turn into your prayers FOR him.

Lastly, I pray God sends him to you **soon**. But most of all, I pray you are both ready.

Blessings,

Cheryl

■ Prologue:

Dear God:
I thank You for the opportunity to come boldly before Your throne to submit my request. I thank You because You said that no good thing would You withhold from me. I thank You for preparing and ministering to my good thing, my king, my future husband.

I thank you for the courage to ask you to send him. I thank you for the wisdom to seek YOU as he seeks me. I thank you that you are preparing each of our hearts for each other. I thank you that You are tailoring him for me and me for him.

I thank You for allowing each of us to fully enjoy, embrace and maximize the gift of singleness while You prepare both of our hearts for the gift of marriage. I pray that our singleness reflects You. I pray that our marriage honors You. I pray our union is one with which You will be pleased. Amen.

Dear Future Husband:
As you read these prayers, please know that I am seeking God not just on my behalf, but know that I have asked Him to birth in me exactly what you need, want and could ever pray for and desire in a wife. Also know that I am praying for you, your future, your success and God's purposed destiny for you.

I don't know who you are. Perhaps we have never met. Just know these prayers are not simply words on paper; they are a reflection of God's heart for you through me.

■ How to get the most out of this devotional

This devotional is written in 31-Day increments. It is meant to be read one day at a time. Because each prayer is short and sweet, I know it will be tempting to simply plow through them at one sitting.

However, I'm going to ask you to take your time. Go through them one at a time and reflect on the meaning behind each prayer. As you read each prayer, I want you to see yourself praying to and for the husband God is preparing for you.

These prayers are not meant to simply be a wish list for your future husband, but your heart's cry for his wellbeing. As you pray these prayers, it is my desire that God begins to birth in you a heart for the man He is sending you.

Let these prayers minister to you. Let these prayers be the beginning of a wellspring of hope as you prepare for the man that God is preparing for you.

You'll find that just as these prayers display your heart for your future husband, God will begin to work on, soften and prepare his heart for you too.

Enjoy!

...a threefold cord is not quickly broken.

Ecclesiastes 4:12b

Day One
Dear Future Husband:

It is likely that I haven't met you yet. But somewhere in my heart I know you are praying for me, looking for me and asking God to prepare you for me. As you pray and seek God for me, know that I am doing the same and asking Him to prepare me for you.

I pray that He would knit our hearts together. I pray that He would fortify us for our journey through life together. I pray that He has equipped me with the complementary skills, gifts and talents that you need to achieve your purpose so that together we can show the world a picture of good success – God's success.

I pray that you don't grow weary in your search. I pray that in your searching for me you aren't manipulated or tricked by the enemy to choose wrong. I pray that God's Spirit nudges, pulls and tugs at your heart until you find me.

When you grow anxious, please gain hope, strength and peace knowing that I am praying for you! Amen.

Two are better than one; because they have a good reward for their labour. For if they fall, the one will lift up his fellow: but woe to him that is alone when he falleth; for he hath not another to help him up.
Ecclesiastes 4:9-10

Day Two
Dear Future Husband:

I pray that when you see me coming, you see help. I pray you see the answer to your prayers. I pray that you find a soft place to lay your head when you feel the world is caving in on you, the path seems ever so dim and the way is hard.

I pray that I am the place you seek comfort and rest. I pray you know that I am someone who will cheer you on in your triumphs, cry with you in life's hard seasons and fight right alongside you through your difficulties.

I pray you see someone with whom you can trust your heart. I pray you see someone who will never knowingly hurt you but who will champion you, support your purpose and goals and help you grow to be all that God has called you to be. Amen.

Love is patient, love is kind. It does not envy, it does not boast, it is not proud. It does not dishonor others, it is not self-seeking, it is not easily angered, it keeps no record of wrongs.

1 Corinthians 13:4-5 NIV

Day Three
Dear Future Husband:

I am not perfect. Sometimes I'm really opinionated, strong-willed, and I think I'm right most of the time. BUT, I am fiercely loyal, supportive and also have a huge heart. I love hard, give generously and enjoy squeezing the most joy I can out of life.

I will not be perfect, but I vow to be willing. Willing to learn how to love you like God loves you. Willing to support and undergird your dreams and goals. Willing to allow you space to grow. Willing to accept the fact that you too are imperfect. But I know with God's grace, as imperfect as we are, we can grow together perfectly. Amen.

*He hath shewed thee, O man, what is good; and what doth the L*ORD *require of thee, but to do justly, and to love mercy, and to walk humbly with thy God?*
Micah 6:8

Day Four
Dear Future Husband:

I pray that you are walking in your purpose and that your life is filled with love and joy BEFORE we meet. I pray you love to travel, see new things and have a zest for living and life.

I pray that you've made a conscious decision to fill each day of your life with as much joy and peace as you can and that you are enjoying the journey.

I pray you are excited about seeking out new adventures, conquering new mountains and that you are looking for someone with whom you can "experience life." Amen.

Rejoice evermore. Pray without ceasing. In every thing give thanks: for this is the will of God in Christ Jesus concerning you.
1 Thessalonians 5:16-18

Day Five
Dear Future Husband:

I pray that you are happy BEFORE I meet you. I pray that you LOVE LIFE, LOVE PEOPLE and most importantly, I pray that you LOVE YOU!

I pray that I'll be a great addition to your already wonderful life and not medicine to soothe a troubled existence.

I pray that God has taught you that you are unique, special and one of His elect, His chosen. I pray you find your confidence in ***GOD*** and are secured by His love. Amen

A merry heart doeth good like a medicine.
Proverbs 17:22a

Day Six
Dear Future Husband:

I pray that you have a sense of humor. I pray that you know how to laugh, have fun and truly enjoy this gift of life God has given us.

I pray that you've discovered how to turn each disappointment into a life lesson that deepens your discernment and increases your wisdom.

I pray your heart is full of joy, despite the difficult seasons we often go through. I pray that during your life, you've learned how to be content in whatever state you're in and have found the formula to love life (which is hoping and resting in Jesus) even when it seems as if life doesn't love you back. Amen.

But whoso keepeth his word, in him verily is the love of God perfected: hereby know we that we are in him.
1 John 2:5

Day Seven
Dear Future Husband:

I pray that you are steady, consistent and a man of your word. I pray that you have firm convictions that you will hold to and not waver despite what others say. I pray you have a true, abiding and foundational relationship with Christ.

I pray that your decision-making strategy includes Christ as your anchor and chief of staff. I pray you consult Him in all you do before moving forward.

I pray that even as you are progressive in your thoughts, you are also steady as a rock in your beliefs. Amen.

I will therefore that men pray everywhere, lifting up holy hands, without wrath and doubting.
I Timothy 2:8

Day Eight
Dear Future Husband:

I pray that you know how to pray. I pray that you know how to reach our Father and that you spend time with Him daily. I pray that your relationship with God brings you the ultimate joy. I pray He knows your name and loves to hear from you.

I pray that your prayer life is consistent and that your talks and conversation with God bring you peace, joy and contentment.

I pray that your time with Him is not ritualistic, but a natural outflow of your acknowledgement that you need Him to direct your steps, comfort your soul and protect those He's entrusted into your care. Amen.

Who can find a virtuous woman? for her price is far above rubies.

Proverbs 31:10

Day Nine
Dear Future Husband:

I pray you have space in your life for me. I pray that I won't simply be an accessory to your life, but a necessary and desired element. I pray you know the value of a wife and have seen great examples of them.

Although your life may seem full and busy, I pray you see the benefit of having a partner to share your thoughts, your fears, and your life's dreams and goals. I pray you see it as a blessed priority and not drudgery.

I pray you have a healthy relationship with your mother, sisters and the women God has placed in your life. I pray you value them as the assets God meant them to be to you. Amen.

Be kindly affectioned one to another with brotherly love; in honour preferring one another.
Romans 12:10

Day Ten
Dear Future Husband:

I pray you value my mind as I will value yours. I pray that you will value my thoughts as I will value yours. I pray my opinion holds weight with you. I pray your heart and mind is open to receive me as your helpmeet and not your arm piece.

I pray we have can have great conversations on topics great and small. I pray we intellectually inspire one another. I pray we can disagree on things without diminishing or belittling one another.

I pray that when our thoughts aren't the same, our respect for one another will be. I pray that you can accept someone whose opinions may not always match yours, but whose heart will always be yours. Amen.

Thou wilt shew me the path of life: in thy presence is fulness of joy; at thy right hand there are pleasures for evermore.
Psalm 16:11

Day Eleven
Dear Future Husband:

I pray that you have a daily, vibrant relationship with Christ. I pray that you see Him as a loving father you find joy in talking to everyday, and not as an escape hatch you use to get you out of troubled times.

I pray that you see Him as your Source of direction, joy and peace. I pray He is the One you go to for encouragement, confidence and peace. I pray He is your steady rock, your refuge and your hiding place.

I pray that you can't imagine life without Him and that your life is a beautiful reflection of your relationship with Him. Amen.

Every good gift and every perfect gift is from above, and cometh down from the Father of lights, with whom is no variableness, neither shadow of turning.
James 1:17

Day Twelve
Dear Future Husband:

I pray that you are kind, sensitive and generous. I pray that you use your position of authority as a tool to help others and not just to enrich yourself. I pray that you never use your influence to demean or belittle others.

I pray that you are neither self-absorbed nor arrogant. I pray that you understand that every gift and every talent you have is a gift from God to bless you and those around you.

I pray that you are unselfish with the use of those gifts. I pray that you are unselfish with your kindness. I pray that you are unselfish with your love. Amen.

Behold, how good and how pleasant it is for brethren to dwell together in unity!
Psalm 133:1

Day Thirteen
Dear Future Husband:

I pray that you understand that more than needing you in my life, I WANT you in my life. I want you to be my friend.

I want you to be my confidant. I want you to be the one I have the most fun with and with whom I can share my heart's disappointments.

I want you to know that you are more than a necessity. I want you to feel and to know that being with you is a JOY! Amen.

The Lord is my shepherd; I shall not want.

Psalm 23:1

Day Fourteen
Dear Future Husband:
___

I pray that you see & recognize God as your ultimate Source. I pray you run to Him when you feel weak and unsure and that you look to Him as your ultimate provider.

I pray He is your Rock. I pray He is your Firm Foundation. I pray He has your heart. I pray that you trust NO ONE like you trust and honor Him.

I pray that you are anchored in your faith, sure of your calling and moving in the path He's set for you! Amen.

To every thing there is a season, and a time to every purpose under the heaven.
Ecclesiastes 3:1

Day Fifteen
Dear Future Husband:

I pray that you are balanced. I pray that your deep relationship with Christ isn't a mask for your deep disappointment with life. I pray that the abundant life you live is simply an overflow of the abundant peace and joy you've found in Christ.

I pray that your recreational life is as solid as your prayer life. I pray you know how to have FUN! I pray that you see fun, excitement and joy as necessary as prayer, Bible study and worship. I pray you have a holistic view of the life Christ died for you to have. And I pray that I will be a beautiful addition to it. Amen.

Whoso findeth a wife findeth a good thing, and obtaineth favour of the LORD.
Proverbs 18:22

Day Sixteen
Dear Future Husband:

I pray you can receive. I pray you can receive God's love to you in the wife He is giving you. I know God has created you to be an awesome giver, but I also pray that He has graced you to be open to receive as well.

I pray you can warmly receive her heart, her wisdom, her kindness and her vulnerabilities. I pray you are ready to fully embrace all she is and all she will become because she is connecting to you. Amen.

A man that hath friends must shew himself friendly: and there is a friend that sticketh closer than a brother.
Proverbs 18:24

Day Seventeen
Dear Future Husband:

I pray that God has connected you with wonderful, honest, trustworthy friends who love, honor and respect who you are as a person. I pray that He's surround you with a God-fearing tribe of believers who support your dreams, honor your life as a believer and cherish your friendship.

I pray they are a group of men with whom you can truly be yourself without fear of jealousy, envy or strife. I pray they are men you can have fun with, seek wisdom from and enjoy time and space in their company. I pray they are friends for life. Amen.

Remember your leaders, who spoke the word of God to you. Consider the outcome of their way of life and imitate their faith.
Hebrews 13:7 NIV

Day Eighteen
Dear Future Husband:

I pray God gives you a mentor who is more like a father/mother to you. One who will pray for you, provide sound wisdom and advice and cover you. I pray he or she is someone you respect, admire and trust.

I pray they have no agenda, no hidden motives or no secret wish to be you. I pray that like Elijah, their only goal is to impart knowledge, wisdom and faith into your life.

I also pray God will send you trusted advisors who speak into your life if you don't currently have it. Men and women of God who have already walked the path you're on right now, who will encourage, uplift and challenge you to be all that God has called you to become. Amen.

Do you not know that your bodies are temples of the Holy Spirit, who is in you, whom you have received from God? You are not your own; you were bought at a price. Therefore honor God with your bodies.
I Corinthians 6:19-20 NIV

Day Nineteen
Dear Future Husband:

I pray for your physical health. I pray you have a regular exercise regimen and do your best to eat right. I pray you have a healthy view of rest. I pray that you intersperse personal play and rest into your work and workout schedule.

I pray you realize your body is one of your most precious assets. I pray you don't idolize it, but I do pray that you take care of it and nurture it. I pray you see it as equally important as your spiritual, emotional and financial health. Amen.

Trust in the Lord with all thine heart; and lean not unto thine own understanding. In all thy ways acknowledge him, and he shall direct thy paths.
Proverbs 3:5-6

Day Twenty
Dear Future Husband:

I pray for your emotional health. I pray that you have a healthy view of life, people and yourself. I pray that God is healing the emotional scars that have wounded and afflicted you over the years.

I pray that those disappointments and discouragements have taught you sensitivity, patience and endurance. I pray that you've learned from those difficult times and haven't been diminished by them. I pray you are stronger, wiser and better because of them. Amen.

But remember the LORD your God, for it is he who gives you the ability to produce wealth, and so confirms his covenant, which he swore to your ancestors, as it is today.
Deuteronomy 8:18 NIV

Day Twenty-One
Dear Future Husband:

I pray for your financial health. I pray that you are fiscally responsible with the finances with which God has blessed you. I pray that you don't misuse resources, but have a healthy respect for money.

I pray you use it wisely. I pray you don't covet it and haven't allowed greed to consume you. I pray you see money for the tool it is. A resource to provide for you and your family, a gift to help others less fortunate than you, a resource to build God's kingdom and a treasure to leave behind for the next generation. Amen.

You will be secure, because there is hope; you will look about you and take your rest in safety. You will lie down, with no one to make you afraid, and many will court your favor.
Job 11:18-19 NIV

Day Twenty-Two
Dear Future Husband:

I pray you are kind, generous and lighthearted. I pray that the cares of the world and the tragedies you may have faced haven't hardened you toward the glorious beauty of life nor blinded you to the great possibilities all around you.

I pray you still have hope and are still able to find joy in the simple pleasures of life like peace, family, friends and a place to call home.

I pray you can shake off the disappointments of yesterday and find hope in the great possibilities today and tomorrow can bring. Amen.

A wise man will hear, and will increase learning; and a man of understanding shall attain unto wise counsels.
Proverbs 1:5

Day Twenty-Three
Dear Future Husband:

I pray you have seen many examples of great marriages. I pray people who honor, esteem and celebrate God's gift of marriage surround you. I pray that even if your parents didn't have a great marriage, their situation has not soured you to the possibility of you having one.

I pray that God shows you how a great marriage can flourish. I pray that He shows you how two people who are deeply committed God and to one another can bring out the best in each person individually, while knitting them together as one. Amen.

I will praise thee; for I am fearfully and wonderfully made: marvellous are thy works; and that my soul knoweth right well.
Psalm 139:14

Day Twenty-Four
Dear Future Husband:

I pray that your confidence and esteem comes from God alone. I pray that you understand that you are great because you are HIS. I pray that no matter how much money you make (or don't make), how big your house is or despite the car you drive, I pray your identity lies in the fact that you belong to God.

I pray you know and feel His unconditional love for you when you have plenty and even when you don't. I pray that you don't measure yourself by man's standard of acquiring "things," but that you know you're worthy because God said so, and I pray you know that is enough. Amen.

The L̇ord will guide you always; he will satisfy your needs in a sun-scorched land and will strengthen your frame. You will be like a well-watered garden, like a spring whose waters never fail.
Isaiah 58:11 NIV

Day Twenty-Five
Dear Future Husband:

I pray you are walking in perpetual overflow. I pray you have more than enough for yourself so you can now give to others. I pray that your life is so full and so rich that you are looking for ways to bless others.

I pray you have more than enough money, more than enough wisdom, more than enough confidence, more than enough fun, and more than enough life to share with me and with those God has called you to reach. Amen.

For where two or three are gathered together in my name, there am I in the midst of them.
Matthew 18:20

Day Twenty-Six
Dear Future Husband:

I am so thankful to God that you are secure in who you are as a man. I'm thankful that you are not intimidated to be with a God-fearing woman who has a call and assignment on her life.

I am thankful that you champion and encourage the gift of God on the inside of me because you know that God sent me to be a blessing to you and the earth. I thank you for seeing my calling not as an affront or hindrance to your call or greatness, but as a great complement to it. I thank you for seeing us as a team and not competitors. I thank you for having the grace to walk with someone who is also anointed and who is divinely appointed to be yours. Amen.

And be ye kind one to another, tenderhearted, forgiving one another, even as God for Christ's sake hath forgiven you.
Ephesians 4:32

Day Twenty-Seven
Dear Future Husband:

I pray you have a forgiving, trusting heart – because I'll need it. I pray that you are not easily wounded and that you don't hold grudges. I pray that if and when I hurt or wound you, you easily forgive.

I pray that during those times of hurt, you know that my heart for you has never wavered, but is always FOR YOU even in my shortcomings. I pray you know it is never my desire to intentionally hurt you, but because I am human, it is likely that I will.

I pray that during these moments, you see me through God's eyes and love me with His heart. Amen.

I have shewed you all things, how that so labouring ye ought to support the weak, and to remember the words of the Lord Jesus, how he said, It is more blessed to give than to receive.
Acts 20:35

Day Twenty-Eight
Dear Future Husband:

I pray you are kind, resilient and trustworthy. I pray you have a kind, generous heart and spirit. I pray that giving is second nature to you and is something that makes your heart sing.

I pray that you see the gifts, talents and resources God has entrusted you with as bounty not just for you, but for the many people He will put in your path. I pray you know that you are a generous distribution center for God and that the more you give, the more He'll give back to you. Amen.

And over all these virtues put on love, which binds them all together in perfect unity.
Colossians 3:14 NIV

Day Twenty-Nine
Dear Future Husband:

I pray that God will knit our hearts together. I pray that our heartbeats, though they are two separate and distinct hearts, synchronize and beat in harmony and rise as beautiful music to the One who created and joined us together.

I pray that you know you don't have to be "like" me for you to love you. I also pray that you don't require me to be just "like" you for you to love me. I pray that our differences are complementary and help us love and appreciate the unique gift we have in each other. I pray we recognize that it's what makes our love special. Amen.

For which of you, intending to build a tower, sitteth not down first, and counteth the cost, whether he have sufficient to finish it? Lest haply, after he hath laid the foundation, and is not able to finish it, all that behold it begin to mock him, Saying, This man began to build, and was not able to finish.
Luke 14:28-30

Day Thirty
Dear Future Husband:

I pray that you are ready. I pray you have counted up the cost of leaving singleness to be connected to another beautifully flawed, but incredibly graced individual. I pray you feel you've fully completed your season of singleness. I pray you've learned who you are, whose you are and who God is calling you to be during that time.

I also pray that you've learned the kind of woman you desire to walk with you in your season of marriage. I pray you've selected those attributes through thoughtful times of prayer and communion with Christ. I pray you were honest with what you need AND what you desire in a wife. I pray you are ready to receive her with joy. Amen.

...For this cause shall a man leave father and mother, and shall cleave to his wife: and they twain shall be one flesh? Wherefore they are no more twain, but one flesh. What therefore God hath joined together, let not man put asunder.
Matthew 19:5-6

Day Thirty-One
Dear Future Husband:

I pray you are excited about life with me. I pray that you are looking forward to sharing your life, your wisdom, your faith, and your heart with the person God has set aside just for you – *me*.

I pray marriage is something you believe in, have faith in and are looking forward to being a vital part of. I pray you are ready. Amen.

Other Great Books by Cheryl

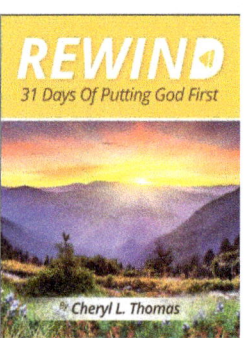

Cheryl has penned several books to enhance the daily walk of Christians everywhere so that people of faith can live the best life ever.

Feel free to visit her website www.CherylThomas.co/Store to secure a copy of one her other books today.

DOWNLOAD A FREE VIDEO SERIES

READ THIS FIRST

Just to say THANKS for downloading my book, I would like to give you a FREE video series of the behind the scenes of "The Making of Dear Future Husband," 100% FREE!!!

CLICK HERE TO DOWNLOAD

(Or go to www.CherylThomas.co/DFH-FreeVideos)

So...you want to know who I am.

I am a dreamer, purpose motivator, personal empowerment coach, minister and child of God. It is my heart's desire and passion to help you BE who God created you to be so you can DO what God created you to do.

You see, I believe you have to know who God says you are first, BEFORE you can do what He you created to do. It is a journey in self discovery, which ultimately leads to personal & professional fulfillment.

And contrary to popular belief, it can be FUN!

My purpose in life is to help you recover your faith so you can walk in your purpose & live the fun, exciting life you were meant to live. Are you ready to live? Your presence here shows me you are. Know that with God on your side, you will win!

Website: www.CherylThomas.co
Email: Cheryl@CherylThomas.co

www.ingramcontent.com/pod-product-compliance
Lightning Source LLC
Chambersburg PA
CBHW071404160426
42813CB00083B/439